Southern Living

simple

FLOWER

arranging

Southern Living

simple

FLOWER

arranging

Oxmoor House

Southern Living® Simple Flower Arranging
©2001 by Oxmoor House, Inc.
Book Division of Southern Progress Corporation
P.O. Box 2463, Birmingham, AL 35201

Created especially for *Southern Living At HOME™*,
the Direct Selling Division of Southern Progress Corporation

Library of Congress Control Number: 00-091846
ISBN: 0-8487-2559-X
Printed in the United States of America
First Printing 2001

We're here for you! We at Oxmoor House are dedicated to serving you with reliable
information that expands your imagination and enriches your life.
We welcome your comments and suggestions. Please write us at:
Oxmoor House, Inc.,
Editor, Southern Living® Simple Flower Arranging
2100 Lakeshore Drive,
Birmingham, AL 35209
To order additional publications, call 1-205-445-6560.
For more books to enrich your life, visit
oxmoorhouse.com

Oxmoor House, Inc.
Editor-in-Chief: Nancy Fitzpatrick Wyatt
Executive Editor: Susan Carlisle Payne
Art Director: Cynthia Rose Cooper

Southern Living At HOME™
Vice President and Executive Director: Dianne Mooney
Design Associate: Melanie Grant

Southern Living® Simple Flower Arranging
Editor: Lauren Caswell Brooks
Designer: Melissa Clark
Copy Editor: Jacqueline Giovanelli
Editorial Assistant Interns: Megan Graves, Lindsey Hanes
Senior Photographer: Jim Bathie
Photographers: Jean Allsopp, Ralph Anderson, Van Chaplin, Tina Cornett,
Laurey W. Glenn, Brit Huckabay, Sylvia Martin
Senior Photo Stylist: Kay E. Clarke
Photo Stylists: Buffy Hargett, Mary Lyn Jenkins, Leslie Byars Simpson
Contributing Photo Stylist: Susan Huff
Director, Production and Distribution: Phillip Lee
Production Coordinator: Leslie Wells Johnson
Production Assistant: Faye Porter Bonner

CONTENTS

flower
PRIMER

Follow our tips for cutting, conditioning, and caring for your flowers to maximize the impact of your arrangements.

Floral foam comes in all shapes and sizes. Let the foam stand in water until it's completely saturated before inserting stems.

Having the right tools makes flower arranging a snap. Shown are: clippers, florist tape, pipe cleaners, picks, water picks, wire, chicken wire, and a floral frog.

Using a knife, remove the thorns from rose stems, working from the top down. If you use roses often, you might want to invest in a stem stripper.

Cut flower stems at an angle ▶ so they absorb water better. It's also easier to insert angled stems in floral foam.

To help woody stems absorb water, crush each stem end with a hammer. Next, cut a slit several inches long with a knife. ▼

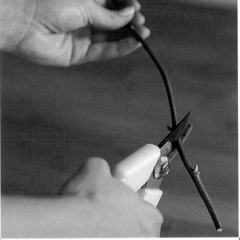

▲ Before arranging flowers, remove excess foliage. A few leaves give flowers a natural appearance, but too many will detract from the bouquet. Remove all leaves that will be under water. If left on, they will breed bacteria and shorten the life of the arrangement.

Fill a water pick with water, ▶ and push the stem through the hole in the cap. Insert the pick directly into an arrangement, floral foam, or a potted plant. This small reservoir of water helps keep the flower hydrated.

CREATIVE CONTAINERS

Choose a vase that complements the arrangement in size and style. Browse through cabinets and closets for out-of-the-ordinary containers. Don't hesitate to use items not traditionally used for floral arranging. If a container will not hold water or is very large, place a jar or cup inside to hold the flowers.

CUTTING FROM THE GARDEN

When cutting flowers from your garden, bring along a container of water and sharp clippers. A clean cut made with a sharp tool enables water to travel up the stem into the flower head, prolonging the life of the bloom. Dull clippers crush the stem. Choose blossoms that are newly opened and buds just beginning to unfurl. Cut flowers one at a time, and immediately place each stem in water. Condition flowers by soaking them in lukewarm water for a few hours in a cool, dark place. Soak the florist foam in water until it's completely saturated. Cut each stem again under water before you add it to the arrangement; this enables water instead of air to travel up the stem. If you've only cut a few flowers, recut the stems under a running faucet. For a larger bouquet, cut stems under a small amount of water in the sink or a wide container. After arranging, add a floral preservative to the water. An alternative is to add one or two drops of chlorine bleach and 1 teaspoon sugar per quart of water. Replenish the water daily, and recut the stems after several days.

ORDERLY ARRANGEMENTS

•Simple bouquets are the most appealing. Interest comes from varying flower shapes and colors. Bouquets need not be large, but cut flowers should be of similar size.

•Feel free to supplement garden flowers with blooms purchased from a florist for variety.

•Cut garden flowers early in the morning before it gets hot.

•Arrange the tallest stems first so they set an outline for the bouquet.

•Insert taller flowers in the center, and fill in with flowers that become progressively shorter as you near the edges of the container.

•To keep an arrangement from wilting, place it away from direct sunlight.

spring

FLOWERS IN A HANGING BASKET

This springtime arrangement is perfect for hanging on a door or wall.

use: moss, roses, kermit mums

1. Cut a block of floral foam to fit down inside the basket.

2. Soak the foam in water, and place it in a plastic zip-top bag.

3. Arrange some moss in the front of the basket, and set the bag with foam in the basket behind the moss.

4. Insert the roses at different angles in the foam. Fill in open spaces with kermit mums.

5. Tie some ribbon to a floral pick with wire, and make a bow. Insert the pick in the foam on one side of the basket.

———

For variety, use several colors of roses in the arrangement.

Substitute daisies or another spring flower if roses aren't available.

FLORAL MEDLEY IN AN IRON CONSERVATORY

Moss and flowers can embellish simple garden accessories.

*use: moss, roses, larkspur, scabiosis, lamb's-ear, stock,
variegated vinca, sedum, lantana*

1. Wet the moss, and place it in the floor of the conservatory.

2. Soak an adhesive-backed small floral foam dome in water.

3. Insert the roses, larkspur, scabiosis, lamb's-ear, stock, and
   variegated vinca into the foam.

4. Place the dome in one of the conservatory's corners.

5. Weave additional vinca up the side of the conservatory.

6. Fill in open spaces with sedum and lantana.

*You can create a small flower arrangement similar to this in an
adhesive-backed small floral dome and use it as a package topper.*

LILIES AND ROSES IN A SILVER BOWL

Flowers of similar hues create a stunning monochromatic centerpiece.

use: lilies, roses

1. Cut a block of floral foam to fit inside the bowl.

2. Soak the foam in water, and place it in the bowl.

3. Insert the full-blooming lilies in the foam, and fill in open spaces with roses and lilies with closed buds.

Stamen-bearing pollen inside the lilies will stain clothing.
To remove the pollen, wipe the inside of the flower with a pipe cleaner
(see below).

ROSES ON A CANDLESTICK

These candlesticks make an elegant centerpiece
that won't block your guests' view of each other.

use: roses, ivy

Step 3

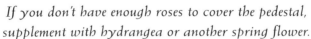
Step 6

1. Soak a floral foam pedestal in water.

2. Place the pedestal on top of the candlestick.

3. Cut the stems of the roses short, and insert the roses into the pedestal to cover. Leave a space for the candle in the top center of the pedestal.

4. Insert one piece of ivy into the top of the pedestal and one piece into the bottom.

5. Place a candle in the top center of the pedestal.

6. Cut the stem of one rose completely off. Remove the center rose petals, and place a tea light candle inside the flower. Put the rose and candle in a cup.

If you don't have enough roses to cover the pedestal,
supplement with hydrangea or another spring flower.

SPRING FLOWERS IN CONES

Ideal for hanging on chairbacks or doorknobs, these cone vases bring spring inside.

use: roses, kermit mums, scabiosis, stock, hydrangea

1. Cut a block of floral foam to fit inside each of the cones.

2. Soak the foam in water, and place in the cones.

3. For each cone, take a few stems of each flower, except hydrangea, and gather them to form a small bouquet, called a tussie mussie. Wrap a pipe cleaner around the stems to secure the bouquet.

4. Insert the tussie mussie into a cone. Tuck hydrangea in the front of the cone to fill any open spaces.

5. Tie a bow made of ribbon to the cone, and secure the cone to the chair.

Step 3

*If your cones are watertight, simply pour water
into the cones instead of using floral foam.*

TULIPS IN A VASE

*The graceful curve of tulip stems adds to the beauty of their arrangement.
The top of this vase has about 20 holes—similar to a floral frog—that guides
placement of the flowers and anchors them in the vase.*

use: tulips

1. Insert a tulip into each of the holes in the top of the container.

———

*Refrigerate the tulips until just before you plan to use
them so they stay fresh.*

*To give volume at the base and add more color to the arrangement,
leave some foliage on the stalks of the tulips.*

*If your vase doesn't have a lid with holes, place a floral frog in
the bottom of the vase. Insert stems in the holes for extra stability.*

FLOWER BASKET IN A BUBBLE GLASS BOWL

*This basket-inspired arrangement rests in a simple bowl vase.
Stems of larkspur inserted on either side of the vase meet in the center
above the flowers to resemble a basket handle.*

use: moss, roses, kermit mums, stock, lavender, pachysandra, larkspur

1. Cut a block of floral foam to fit inside the bowl.

2. Soak the foam in water, and place in the bowl.

3. Arrange some moss in the front and sides of the bowl so the foam doesn't show.

Step 5

4. Insert the roses, kermit mums, stock, lavender, and pachysandra at different angles into the foam.

5. Insert larkspur on either side of the foam, and bring together to make a handle to resemble a basket. Using a green pipe cleaner, wire the larkspur together.

6. Tie a bow made of ribbon to the larkspur handle.

*Use a green pipe cleaner to wire the larkspur together so it
will blend in with the color of the stems.*

DAFFODILS IN A CONTAINER

Daffodils tied into a cluster provide a sunburst of color.

use: daffodils, moss

1. Remove several leaves from one bunch of daffodils. Set aside two leaves.

2. Tie raffia around the top, middle, and bottom of the stems to hold the bundle together.

3. Push the daffodil stems into a small container so they will stand securely.

4. Gently tie the two reserved leaves in a knot over the raffia in the middle.

5. If the container is watertight, add water.

6. Put the container in a square base or other larger container. Place moss at the base of the stems around the container.

Daffodil stalks won't penetrate florist foam easily, so use another kind of container to hold them. If you put them in a vase, put glass marbles in the bottom to hold the stems in place.

FLOWERS IN A SYMPHONY OF CYLINDERS

*Multiple bud vases can transform a modest
bouquet from the grocery store into a beautiful arrangement.*

use: iris, freesia, asters

1. Fill each cylinder with water.

2. Remove excess foliage from the flower stems.

3. Insert the iris, freesia, and asters into the cylinders.

———

*Place the cylinders on a tray to unify the
grouping and to make it portable.*

LILAC IN A COFFEEPOT

*A vase can be as simple as an accessory in your kitchen,
such as this striking enamel coffeepot.*

use: lilac

1. Cut a block of floral foam to fit inside the coffeepot.

2. Soak the foam in water, and place in the coffeepot.

3. Insert the lilac at different angles into the foam.

———

*Since coffeepots are typically watertight, you could fill one with water instead
of using floral foam. The foam, however, helps the arrangement keep its shape.*

FLOWERS IN A SILVER BOWL

*This mix of woodsy and delicate flowers proves
that opposites can be attractive together.*

use: tulips, gerbera daisies, acacia, allium, thistle

1. Cut a block of floral foam to fit inside the bowl.

2. Soak the foam in water, and place in the bowl.

3. Insert the tulips, daisies, acacia, and allium into the foam, and
   fill in open spaces with thistle.

—

Using flowers of varying scale adds interest and dimension to an arrangement.

SPRING FLING IN A WICKER BASKET

*Bare branches still visible among these earliest blooms
of spring herald the transition of the seasons.*

use: forsythia, quince

1. Cut a block of floral foam to fit inside the basket.

2. Soak the foam in water, and place in a plastic zip-top bag.

3. Place the bag with foam in the basket.

4. Insert branches of forsythia into the foam. Fill in open
   spaces with quince.

—

*Place the tallest forsythia stems first so they form
an outline for the arrangement.*

FLOWERS IN MINI MUGS

Several silver mugs, each holding a different kind of flower, line up in the center of the table for an easy but elegant centerpiece.

use: bavardia, rosemary, roses

1. Trim the flower stems just long enough so the blooms begin above the mug rim.

2. Fill a mug with water, and insert the bavardia.

3. Place either potted rosemary or rosemary sprigs in a pot.

4. Fill a mug with water, and insert the roses.

Scatter herbs among the mix of flowers for extra aroma and color. Garlic chive blossoms and rose petals sprinkled on the table add charm to the setting.

summer

GERBERA DAISIES IN A STEM CONTAINER

*Stems cover the outside of a container and create
the illusion of flowers thriving without water.*

use: gerbera daisies

1. Place a rubber band around the cylindrical container.

2. Cut the stems from the flowers, leaving enough stem so the flower heads can reach the water once placed in the container.

3. Slide the cut stems under the rubber band, and place the stems around the container until it's covered. Trim the stems even with the mouth of the container.

4. Tie a ribbon to cover the rubber band.

5. Fill the container with water, and insert the flowers.

*We used gerbera daisies because they typically have long, slender stems
without leafy foliage. You could also make this arrangement with Asiatic hybrid lilies,
iris, or other daisies with their foliage removed.*

A pretty ribbon hides the rubber band that holds the stems in place.

SEASHELLS AND LILIES IN A GLASS BELL JAR

This arrangement says summer at the beach, but the materials let you bring summer inside year-round.

use: calla lilies, wheat shafts, bear grass, seashells, cockscomb

1. Fill a glass cylinder with water, and put it in the center of a glass bell jar.

2. Place the lilies, wheat, and grass in the cylinder. Fill in around the cylinder with seashells.

3. Arrange the cockscomb around the edge of the cylinder to cover the base of the arrangement.

4. Put candles in two other glass bell jars, and fill in around the base with seashells.

Step 2

Use some green cockscomb since its texture resembles coral and its color blends well with the other elements.

GARDEN FLOWERS IN A TIN PLANTER

*If you have a good-sized garden, you can enjoy the
mixed and colorful blooms of summer all season.*

*use: zinnias, begonias, liriope berries, lantana,
hydrangea, maidenhair fern*

1. Cut a block of floral foam to fit in the tin.

2. Soak the foam in water, and place in a plastic zip-top bag.

3. Set the bag with foam in the tin.

4. Insert the the larger flowers—zinnias and begonias—in the foam first,
   and then tuck in liriope berries, lantana, hydrangea, and maidenhair fern
   to fill in open spaces.

———

*Look for the stems of purple berries in the center of liriope, or "monkey grass."
These berries add color and texture to an arrangement.*

OUTDOOR GREENERY AND FLOWERS IN TERRA-COTTA POTS

Flowers from the florist can't compare with the variety and style of the blossoms that you can find outside your door.

use: roses, phlox, clematis, hosta, chives, rosemary

1. Cut blocks of floral foam to fit inside each of the terra-cotta pots.

2. Soak the foam in water, and place in the pots.

3. Insert the roses, phlox, and clematis into the foam, and fill in open spaces with the tops of hosta, chive blooms, and rosemary.

Step 3

To achieve a similar effect, insert cut flowers in potted plants.

SUMMER BOUQUET IN A GLASS VASE

*Built around a pink and purple color scheme, this arrangement
uses only a few stems of each flower.*

use: zinnias, coneflower, phlox, verbena, veronica, dill blossoms

1. Fill the vase with water.

2. Insert the larger flowers—zinnia, coneflower, and phlox—into
   the vase. Fill in open spaces with verbena, veronica, and
   dill blossoms.

———

*For another way to arrange the bouquet, gather the flowers in your
hand before placing them in a vase. Start with a few stems and add
more, one at a time. Hold the bouquet at arm's length, and see how the
flowers fit together. If a bloom is out of place, gently pull it out from
the top. Once you have a pleasing bouquet, use your free hand to cut
the stems the same length. Place the bouquet in the vase. Loosen the
cluster to fill the container, and add more flowers as needed.*

GREEN BLOOMS AND CONTAINER

Blooms and a container in matching shades add a burst of color to your tabletop.

use: calla lilies, fern, Bells-of-Ireland, Queen Anne's lace, grapes

1. Fill the container with water.

2. Insert the lilies, fern, and Bells-of-Ireland into the container first.
   Fill in open spaces with Queen Anne's lace.

3. Insert a small bunch of grapes into the front of the container.
   Allow them to drape over the side and bend naturally.

———

*Adding a cluster of green grapes brings an unexpected
element to the arrangement.*

DAISIES IN MIXING BOWLS

*Tiered mixing bowls as vases create height and
fullness in this homespun centerpiece.*

use: daisies

1. Cut blocks of floral foam to fit inside three different sizes of mixing bowls.

2. Soak the foam in water, and place in the bowls.

3. Cut the daisies' stems to about 4 inches in length.

4. Insert the daisies into the foam in the smallest bowl to cover.

5. With the biggest bowl on the bottom, stack the bowls one on top of another.

6. Insert the daisies into the foam in the other bowls to cover.

—

Consider using only one color of daisy for a monochromatic arrangement.

CONEFLOWERS IN A WOODEN BOWL

An old wooden dough bowl holds an earthy arrangement made from just a few simple coneflowers, moss, and fresh artichokes.

use: coneflower, Spanish moss, artichokes

1. Cut a block of floral foam to fit in the wooden bowl. Soak the foam in water, and place in the bowl.

2. Insert the coneflowers into the foam at different heights.

3. Arrange the moss at the base to cover the foam.

4. Add different sizes of artichokes as accents.

—

To add interest, use coneflowers with varying curved petals. For more color, leave most of the foliage on the coneflowers.

ORANGE FLOWERS IN A GLASS PITCHER

*Orange slices accent the glass pitcher and hide the flower stems.
Lemon and lime slices offer other monochromatic color schemes.*

use: orange slices, gerbera daisies, lilies, tulips

1. Fill the glass pitcher with water and orange slices.

2. Gather the flowers in your hand, arrange them as desired,
   and place them in the pitcher.

—

*If a stem curves in a certain direction, let it bend over the side
of the container; just let flowers do what they naturally do.*

HYDRANGEAS IN A STRIPED VASE

It's easy to extend the enjoyment of this graceful shrub by cutting and even drying the blooms for display indoors.

use: *hydrangeas*

1. Fill the vase with water.

2. Remove leaves from the stems, and place the hydrangeas in the vase.

———

To lengthen your enjoyment of hydrangeas, dry them. Remove all the leaves, and tie the stems in loose bundles. Hang the bundles upside down in a dark, dry place. Another method for drying blooms is to let them stand in an inch of water until it evaporates. Always cut a few more stems than are required for the arrangement as some blooms dry prettier than others.

YELLOW BLOOMS IN A HANGING BASKET

This bright arrangement hanging on your door gives guests a cheerful welcome.

use: gerbera daisies, freesia, stock, solidago, butterfly bush

1. Cut blocks of floral foam to fit in the basket.

2. Soak the foam in water, and place in a plastic zip-top bag.

3. Set the bag with foam in the basket.

4. Insert the larger flowers—daisies, freesia, and stock—into the foam first, and tuck in solidago and butterfly bush to fill in open spaces.

Arrange flowers from the back of the basket towards the front to ensure a full arrangement. Use taller flowers first, and end with shorter flowers in front.

FLOWERS ON A CAKE STAND

*Showcasing an arrangement under glass highlights
the beauty of each bloom.*

*use: anemones, ranunculus, roses, phlox, kermit mums,
wax flowers, lemon slice*

1. Cut a three-inch cube of florist foam, and soak it in water.

2. Place the cube in the center of a glass cake stand. Cut flower stems to about 2 to 3 inches in length, and insert them into the foam. If desired, insert a toothpick in a slice of lemon, and use it as an accent.

3. View the arrangement from all sides to make sure that it looks complete and that foam isn't visible.

4. Add the glass dome.

*Because the flowers receive increased attention, use those in
superb condition with no evident brown spots or creased petals.*

BLACK-EYED SUSANS IN AN ANTIQUE TIN

*A bundle of several types of black-eyed Susans nestles
in a pint-sized mason jar hidden in a tin.*

use: variety of black-eyed Susans

1. Find a container that will fit inside the tin.

2. Fill the container with water.

3. Put the container inside the tin, and place the flowers in the
   container.

—

*When you cut flowers from the garden, choose newly opened
blossoms and select buds that are just beginning to unfurl. Cut flowers
one at a time, and immediately place each stem in water.*

autumn

YARROW AND APPLES IN A VASE

*Summer's warmth and autumn's cool meet in this simple arrangement
of dried flowers, fresh foliage, and luscious fruit.*

use: *dried yarrow, Japanese andromeda, green apples*

Step 3

Step 6

Step 7

1. Cut a block of floral foam to fit inside the vase.

2. Soak the foam in water, and place in the vase. Fill the
   vase with water.

3. Cut a length of chicken wire to mold over the foam to give
   the stems extra support. Using florist's tape, secure the wire
   to the vase, and reinforce it by placing a second strip
   of tape horizontally over the first.

4. Remove foliage from the dried yarrow, and insert stems into
   the foam.

5. Fill in open spaces underneath the yarrow with Japanese
   andromeda.

6. Insert a stick into the base of each apple. Thread florist wire
   through the apple on both sides, twisting the wire around
   the stick.

7. Insert the sticks into the foam at the base of the arrangement.

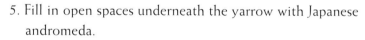

With daily watering, this hearty arrangement should last for up to 10 days.

FALL FLORAL IN A PITCHER

*Dahlias grouped at the base of this autumn arrangement
create a nice focal point.*

use: safflower, hypericum, red solidago, dahlias

1. Fill a pitcher with water.

2. Place the safflower, hypericum, and solidago in the pitcher.

3. Tuck the dahlias in around the edges.

———

*For a fall look, a florist can dye solidago, which is
naturally yellow, and make it red.*

PUMPKIN VASE

You can do much more with a pumpkin than make a pie or carve a jack-o'-lantern—use it as an unexpected container for flowers.

use: pumpkin, lilac, ivy, tulips, euphorbia, gourds

1. Choose a pumpkin that sits upright, slice off its top, and scoop out most of the contents.

2. Select a plastic container small enough to fit through the opening.

3. Cut a block of floral foam to fit inside the container, and soak the block in water.

4. Place the foam in the container, and set both in the pumpkin.

5. Put the top of the pumpkin on a cutting board and, using an apple corer, pierce a dozen holes in it.

6. Set the top on the pumpkin, and insert the flowers and ivy through the holes into the foam, arranging the leaves to cover the holes.

7. Insert sticks into small gourds, and then into the top of the pumpkin.

To protect the table from moisture, display the pumpkin on a ceramic or glass plate.

FLORAL RINGS ON STACKED CAKE PLATES

*Stacking cake plates in graduated sizes extends the
height and grandeur of these wreaths of flowers.*

use: cockscomb, roses, hydrangea, sedum, alstromeria, dahlias, safflower

1. Choose floral foam rings to fit on different sizes of cake plates, and
   soak in water.

2. Place the larger ring on the larger cake plate. Set the smaller cake
   plate in the center of the larger one, and place the smaller ring on top.

3. Cut the stems on the flowers so only a couple of inches remain.

4. Insert the flowers into the floral foam rings to cover.

5. Put a candle in a globe, and set in the center of the smaller cake plate.

Step 4

*If you have only one cake plate, filling one floral foam ring
with flowers still makes an impressive arrangement.*

FLOWERS ON CANDLESTICKS

Rings of autumn flowers draw attention to these stately candlesticks.

use: flowering crabapple, dahlias, red solidago

1. Soak floral foam pedestals in water, and set them on top of the candlesticks.

2. Insert a candle into the center of the each of the pedestals. Insert the crabapple stems into the sides of the pedestal to allow them to hang over the side.

3. Cut the stems of the flowers short. Insert the dahlias into the top and sides of the pedestal, and fill in open spaces with solidago.

Step 2

For a streaming effect, leave some foliage on the crabapple stems.

BITTERSWEET IN AN URN

Combining several kinds of foliage and fruit
will bring a hint of nature indoors.

use: *assorted fall fruit, bittersweet, seeded eucalyptus*

1. Cut a block of floral foam to fit inside the urn.

2. Soak the foam in water, and place in a plastic zip-top bag.

3. Set the bag with foam in the urn.

4. Insert a stick into the base of each piece of fruit, and then in the foam.

5. Fill in open spaces with sprigs of bittersweet and seeded eucalyptus.

—

Group larger fruit first, and then nestle
smaller pieces in the arrangement.

POTTED TOPIARY ON A TRAY

Easy techniques plus elegant flowers equals an impressive arrangement.

use: roses, alstromeria, moss

1. Cut a block of floral foam to fit inside the pot.

2. Soak the foam in water, and place in a plastic zip-top bag. Set the bag with foam in the pot.

3. Cut the roses and alstromeria stems the same length, keeping them as long as possible.

4. Make an alstromeria bouquet, and then add roses around the outside of the bouquet. Tie a green pipe cleaner around the stems to hold the bundle together.

5. Insert the stems into the foam. Arrange the moss around the foam to cover.

6. Wrap ribbon around the stems. Tie a ribbon around the pipe cleaner, and make a bow.

—

Dress up the topiary by wrapping velvet or sheer ribbon around the stems.

GOURD AND ROSES IN AN URN

A collar of roses around the gourd makes this a dressy centerpiece.
A trio of candles in smaller urns accents it nicely.

use: roses, gourd, gerbera daisies

1. Cut a block of floral foam to fit inside the urn.

2. Soak the foam in water, and place in a plastic zip-top bag.

3. Place the bag with foam in the urn.

4. Cut the stems of the roses very short.

5. Set the gourd on top of the foam, and insert the roses in the foam around it.

6. Cut more foam to fit in the smaller urns, soak each in water, and place in a plastic zip-top bag. Place each bag with foam in an urn. Cut the stems of the gerbera daisies short, and insert them into the center of the foam.

7. Wrap raffia bows around small candles, and place on top of the daisies.

If roses aren't available, simply set the gourd in the urn
without using floral foam.

DRIED SPHERES

*Spheres of dried materials make a striking presentation in clusters
as shown or scattered across a mantel.*

use: dried yarrow, celosia, poppy pods, nigella, nuts

1. Set a foam ball in a clay pot.

2. Remove stems from the flowers, and trim close to flower heads. Working with one flower at a time, apply low-melt glue to the base of the flower head, and press it firmly against the ball.

3. Hold it in place until the glue sets. Repeat the process until the ball is covered.

4. Repeat steps with additional foam balls and materials.

*If there is space between the material on the sphere, fill in
the gaps with a complementary color moss.*

HARVEST CENTERPIECE

Your table arrangement becomes a still life of autumn's harvest when you use extra ingredients from Thanksgiving dinner. Herbs, fruits, and vegetables represent seasonal abundance.

use: branches of autumn leaves, dried flowers, sumac, goldenrod, pheasant feathers, sage, sunflower head, pumpkins, nuts, Brussels sprouts, lady apples

1. Arrange the branches of autumn leaves loosely in a container as the focal point for the arrangement.

2. Fill in open spaces with flowers, sumac, goldenrod, and a cluster of pheasant feathers.

3. Arrange additional objects, such as a pitcher and herb-filled terra-cotta pots, at the base of the container to step down in size from the focal point.

4. Fill out the arrangement by using the same materials in additional containers.

5. Place larger elements, such as the sunflower head and pumpkins, close to the focal point. Cluster the smaller pieces—the nuts, Brussels sprouts, and lady apples—on the lowest levels.

The smallest elements belong on the lowest levels, so the arrangement will flow from large to small.

winter

ROSES IN A METAL TIN

*This "gift package" makes a perfect holiday arrangement
for your home or as a present for a friend.*

use: roses, appleberry bush

1. Cut a block of floral foam to fit down inside the tin.

2. Soak the foam in water, and place in a plastic zip-top bag.

3. Place the bag with foam in the tin.

4. Cut the stems of the roses short, and insert into the foam.

5. Fill in open spaces with stems of appleberry bush.

6. Cut two pieces of ribbon long enough to wrap up one side, the bottom, and up another side of the tin. Attach floral picks with wire to the ends of the ribbon.

7. Insert the picks into the foam, and wrap the ribbon around the container so all four sides have ribbon.

8. Fold a long piece of ribbon into loops as shown, pinching the ribbon together at the center. Using a floral pick and wire, secure the loops in the center. Insert the pick in the center of the foam, and fluff the loops as desired.

For a daintier arrangement, use baby's breath instead of appleberry bush.

WINTER WHITE IN RICE PAPER WRAPS

Containers and flowers in the same color palette give this grouping a soothing, clean appearance.

use: star of Bethlehem, cyclamen, Lenten rose, ranunculus

1. Wrap rice paper around jars of varied heights, and use double-stick tape to hold the paper in place.

2. Tie a silk cord around each jar for an elegant touch, if desired.

3. Fill the jars with water.

4. Place the flowers in the jars.

Use one type of flower in each vase, and then group the containers.

LILIES AND KUMQUATS IN A GLASS VASE

Fresh fruit always makes an unexpected and
appealing complement to flowers.

use: lilies, Bells-of-Ireland, kumquat branches

1. Fill the glass vase almost full with water.

2. Insert lilies and Bells-of-Ireland into the vase, and add branches
   of kumquats.

—

Include lilies with closed buds for variety.

BERRIES IN A JULEP CUP

Reminiscent of the South, a mint julep cup makes a classic container.

use: holly berries, pepperberries, seeded eucalyptus

1. Cut a block of floral foam to fit inside the cup.

2. Soak the foam in water, and place in the cup.

3. Remove the leaves from the holly, and insert the stem of the berries in the foam.

4. Insert the pepperberries and seeded eucalyptus into the foam. Allow some of the berries to extend over the side of the cup.

5. Tie a ribbon bow around the neck of the cup, and curl the ends.

—

Create an inexpensive variation of this nosegay by using other small containers such as cans, glass jars, or teacups. With a little bit of ribbon, even a plain jar can be transformed into a container.

TULIPS AND GREENERY IN CHRISTMAS POTTERY

A base of greenery and pomegranates elevates and accents brilliant red tulips.

use: tulips, Leland cypress, seeded eucalyptus, pomegranates, moss

1. Put a full glass of water in the Christmas tree pot, and place the tulips in it.

2. Cut a block of floral foam to fit inside the bowl.

3. Soak the foam in water, and place it in the bowl. Insert Leland cypress, seeded eucalyptus, and pomegranates into the foam, leaving space in the center for the pot of tulips. Place the pot of tulips in the center of the foam in the bowl, and fill in any open spaces in the foam with Leland cypress and seeded eucalyptus.

4. Fill one medium-sized and one small pot with foam. Set a candle on top of the foam in each pot, and insert moss around the base of the candle.

5. Stack one smaller pot inside a medium-sized pot. Place a candle in the smaller pot. Fill in around the edges of both pots with moss.

If you don't have pomegranates, use apples as an accent in this arrangement.

ARTICHOKES AND BERRIES IN AN URN

This elaborate-looking arrangement is a snap to assemble with a simple floral dome cage that shapes and secures the fruit and flowers.

use: greenery, hydrangeas, hypericum, artichokes, pomegranates, pyracantha

1. Cut blocks of floral foam to fit inside the floral dome cage.

2. Soak the foam in water, and place in the urn. Set the dome cage on top of the foam.

3. Insert the greenery, hydrangeas, and hypericum into the foam, leaving the spikes on the dome cage exposed.

4. Cut the artichoke stems short, and push them and the pomegranates onto the spikes.

5. Fill in open spaces with greenery and pyracantha.

This floral dome cage is available from florists, craft stores, and mail-order catalogs.

ANEMONES IN A CHEST

Unexpected items, such as this chest, make striking containers.

use: anemones, holly berries, greenery

1. Cut a block of floral foam to fit inside the chest.

2. Soak the foam in water, and place in a plastic zip-top bag.

3. Place the bag with foam in the chest.

4. Insert the anemones into the foam first. Fill in open spaces with holly berries and greenery.

Step 4

Always line nontraditional containers with a plastic bag to protect the inside.

AMARYLLIS IN AN IRON URN

*The height of amaryllis complements the stately candlestick, and
the mirror behind them multiplies their impact.*

use: amaryllis, moss, fern

1. Set pots of amaryllis in an urn. To help support the flowers, tie the
   stems to bamboo stakes with raffia or hemp.

2. Cut a block of floral foam to fit across the tops of the pots.

3. Soak the foam in water, and place in the urn across the tops of the pots.

4. Place moss around the top edge of the urn.

5. Insert fern into the foam to cover.

———

*Fragrant amaryllis is ideal for creating an inviting
atmosphere for a home's entrance.*

POINSETTIAS IN GLASS CONTAINERS

*Unique containers of varying sizes
showcase poinsettia's vibrant color.*

use: *Spanish moss, poinsettias*

1. Line the bottom of the glass containers with moss.

2. Remove each poinsettia from its pot, and place in the glass containers on top of the moss.

3. Fill in around the roots with potting soil and moss.

—

Place the arrangement in bright, but not direct, sunlight for at least six hours a day. Keep the soil moist with lukewarm water.

A quality poinsettia will have tightly clustered buds with no evidence of pollen on the leaves.

GARDEN GREENERY IN A TERRA-COTTA JAR

*Greenery from your garden can provide varied color, unique
texture, and a pleasing aroma to an arrangement.*

*use: English yew, wax myrtle, holly, bearsfoot hellebore,
leaves of Lenten rose*

1. Place a full glass of water in the terra-cotta jar.

2. Arrange the greenery as desired in the glass inside the jar.

———

*Snipping greenery from trees and shrubs has the same effect
as pruning them; consequently, always cut above a bud, and avoid
leaving stubs. Make cuts at a 45-degree angle, following
the direction of the bud's new growth.*

INDEX

MEANINGFUL BOUQUETS

Besides their aesthetic appeal, flowers can also be tokens of sentiment. The meanings behind flowers, as defined below, are generally based on folklore, mythology, and medicine.

Red rose: *love, Christmas passion, joy, charm*

White rose: *unity, love, respect*

Carnation: *admiration, ardent and pure love, beauty*

Baby's breath: *pure heart, festivity, gaiety*

Peppermint: *warmth of feeling, cordiality*

Rosemary: *devotion, remembrance, wisdom, good luck in the new year*

Parsley: *festivity, gratitude*

Ivy: *fidelity, friendship, constancy*

Holly: *goodwill, domestic happiness*

Berry: *Christmas joy, protection*

Pine: *loyalty, vigorous life, longevity*

Lily: *friendship, pleasantries*

Camellia: *destiny*

Larkspur: *ardent attachment*

Pansy: *thoughts*

Star-of-Bethlehem: *reconciliation*